D0575186

RAINBOW OF ANIMALS

WHY ARE ANIMALS YELLOW?

FREE Educator's Guide AVAILABLE AT ENSLOW.COM

Melissa Stewart

Series Literacy Consultant:
Allan A. De Fina, PhD
Past President of the New Jersey Reading Association
Dean, College of Education/Professor of Literacy Education, New Jersey City University

Series Science Consultant:
Helen Hess, PhD
Professor of Biology
College of the Atlantic
Bar Harbor, Maine

Contents

Words to Know

attract (uh TRAKT)—To make interested; to get the attention of.

blend in—To match; to look the same as.

poison (POY zun)—A material that makes an animal sick. Sometimes the animal gets so sick that it dies.

predator (PREH duh tur)—An animal that hunts and kills other animals for food.

prey (PRAY)—An animal that is hunted by a predator.

survive (sur VYV)—To stay alive.

A Rainbow of Animals

northern cardinal

yellow boxfish

panther chameleon

poison dart frog

Go outside and look around. How many kinds of animals do you see? Rabbits and birds are animals. So are spiders and insects.

Animals come in all sizes and shapes. And they come in all the colors of the rainbow.

leaf-mimic katydid

lesser purple emperor butterfly

Yellow Animals Near You

Can you think of some yellow animals that live near you? Some butterflies are yellow. So are some birds.

Yellow animals live in other parts of the world too. Let's take a look at some of them.

poison dart frog

Go outside and look around. How many kinds of animals do you see? Rabbits and birds are animals. So are spiders and insects.

Animals come in all sizes and shapes. And they come in all the colors of the rainbow.

leaf-mimic katydid

lesser purple emperor butterfly

Yellow Animals Near You

Can you think of some yellow animals that live near you? Some butterflies are yellow. So are some birds.

Yellow animals live in other parts of the world too. Let's take a look at some of them.

tiger swallowtail butterfly

Cup Moth Caterpillars

Some yellow animals are easy to spot. Their bright colors say, "Stay away!" If a hungry bird grabs one of these caterpillars, it will be sorry. The caterpillar's yellow spines give a painful sting.

Fire Salamander

This animal's bright colors send the same message. They tell enemies that the salamander's skin is full of poison. If an animal bites the salamander, it starts to feel sick. It drops the prey and leaves it alone.

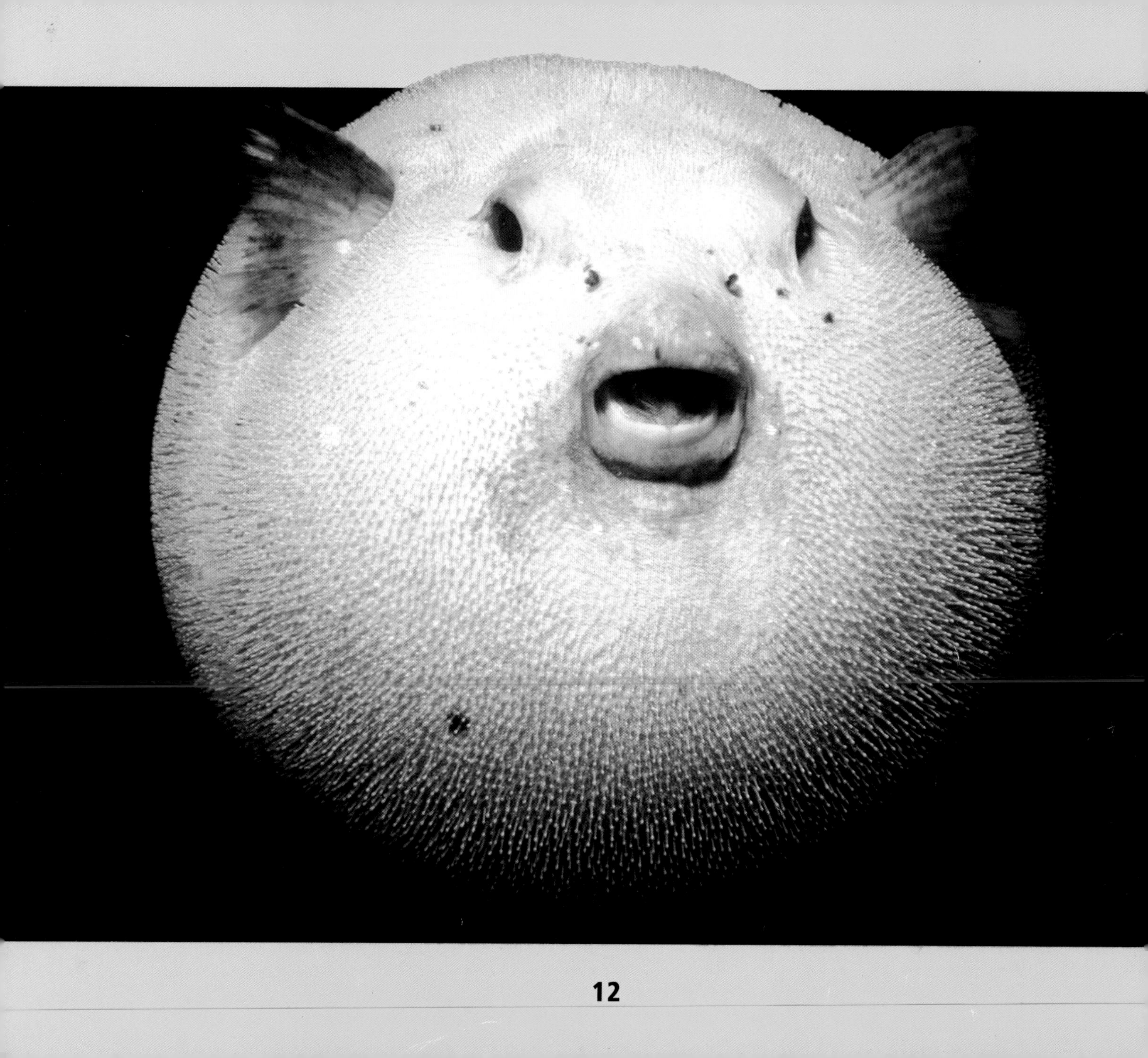

Guineafowl (GIH nee foul) Pufferfish

This fish's bright colors do not always scare enemies. But the fish has another trick for staying safe. If an enemy gets too close, the fish blows up like a balloon. That makes it hard to bite.

Honeybee

A bee's black and yellow stripes say, "Stay away." If a bee feels scared, it stabs its enemy with its stinger. Ouch! That hurts! Poison in the stinger makes skin swell and itch.

American Goldfinch

Some animals want to send out a different message. Their yellow bodies say, "Come to me!"

In summer, a male goldfinch has bright yellow feathers. They help him **attract** a mate. In winter, he gets new feathers. They are brown to **blend in** with his grassy home.

African Lion

Being yellow helps some animals hide. When a lion lies down in the yellow grass, its yellow fur makes it hard to see. This helps it catch prey by surprise.

Canada Goose

This chick's first feathers are fluffy and yellow. They match the color of the dried grass in its nest. That helps the chick stay safe in a world full of predators.

Leafy Sea Dragon

This is not a clump of seaweed. It is a fish. But its yellow color and leaf-like shape fool most predators. A leafy sea dragon floats most of the time. But it can turn using tiny fins on its head.

Great Horned Owl

It can be hard to see in the middle of the night. But light from the moon and stars bounces off the yellow part of this owl's eyes. That makes it easier for the owl to spot rabbits, mice, and other prey.

Guessing Game

Being yellow helps many kinds of animals survive in the world. It helps some animals send a message to mates or predators. It helps other animals hide from their enemies. How do you think being yellow helps the animals in these photos?

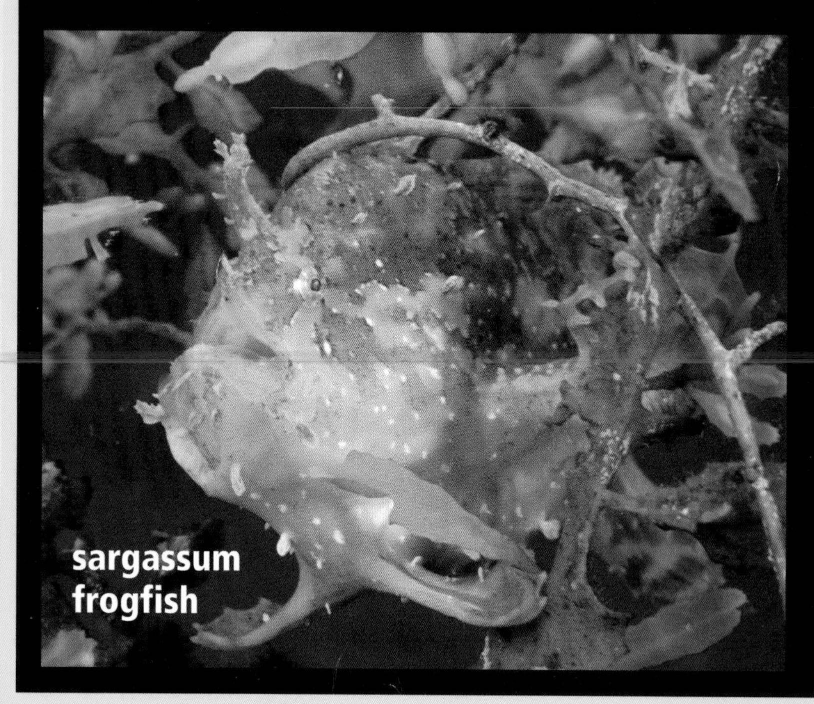
sargassum frogfish

(See answers on page 32.)

eyelash
viper

Where Do These Yellov

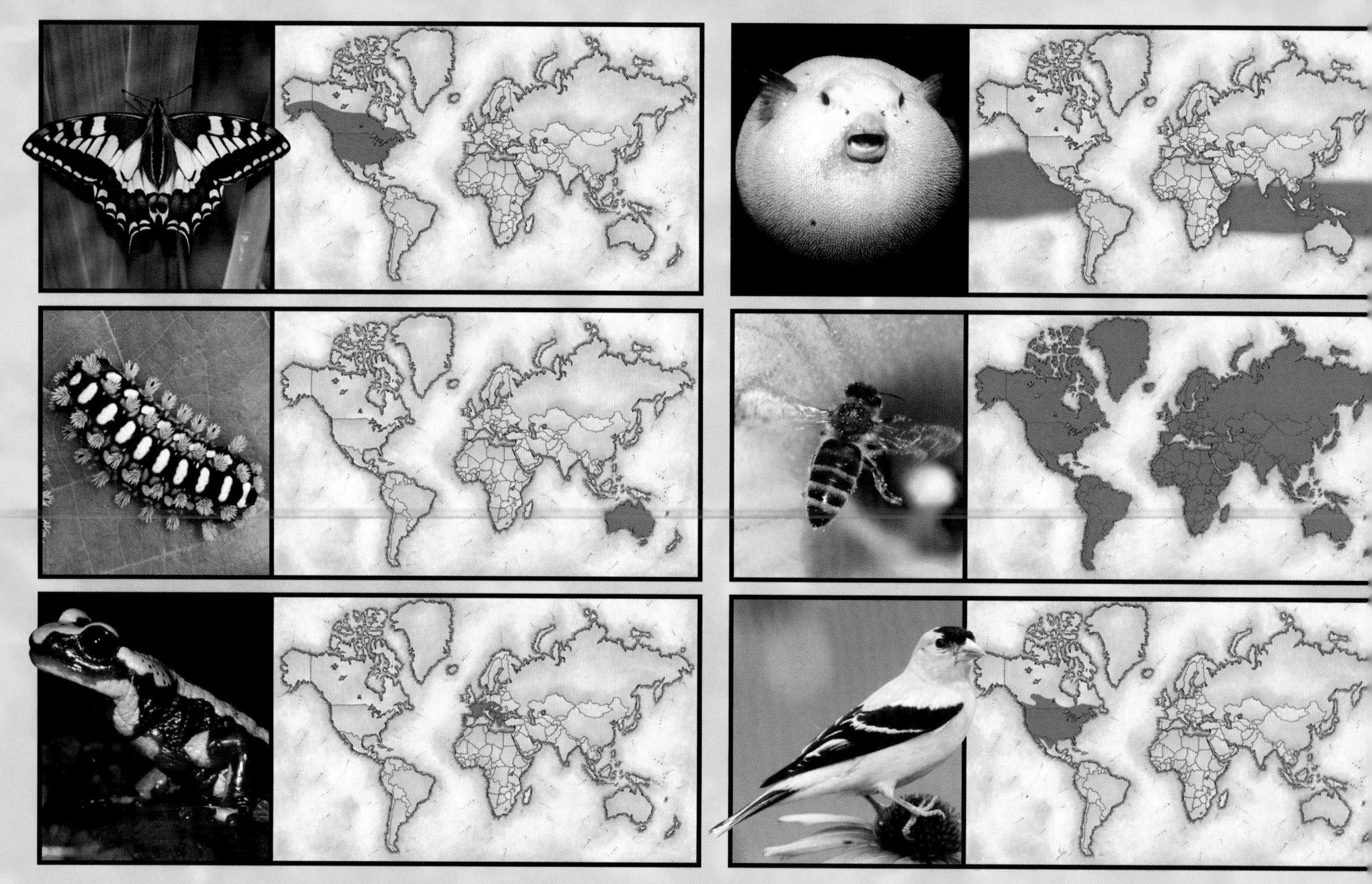

Animals Live?

KEY:
The orange areas on each map below show where that animal lives.

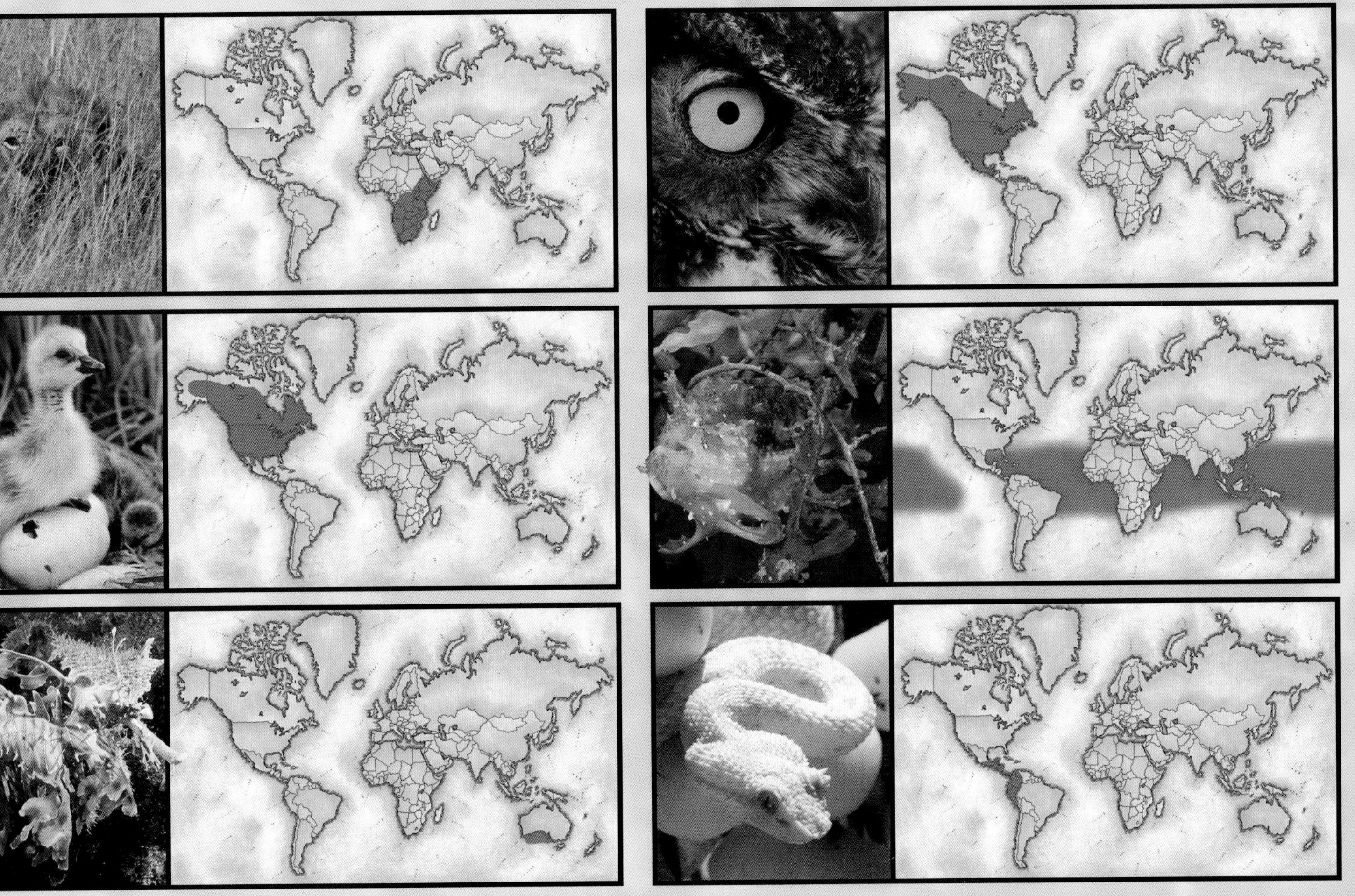

Learn More

Books

Arnosky, Jim. *I See Animals Hiding*. New York: Scholastic, 2000.

Jenkins, Steve. *Living Color*. Boston: Houghton Mifflin, 2007.

Kalman, Bobbie, and John Crossingham. *Camouflage: Changing to Hide*. New York: Crabtree Publishing, 2005.

Stockland, Patricia. *Red Eyes or Blue Feathers: A Book About Animal Colors*. Minneapolis: Picture Window Books, 2005.

Whitehouse, Patricia. *Colors We Eat: Yellow Foods*. Chicago: Heinemann, 2004.

Learn More

Web Sites

Animal Colors

http://www.highlightskids.com/Science/Stories/SS1000_animalColors.asp

Beasts Playground: Camouflage Game

http://www.abc.net.au/beasts/playground/camouflage.htm

How Animal Camouflage Works

http://science.howstuffworks.com/animal-camouflage1.htm

Index

Enslow Elementary, an imprint of Enslow Publishers, Inc.

Enslow Elementary® is a registered trademark of Enslow Publishers, Inc.

Library of Congress Cataloging-in-Publication Data

Stewart, Melissa.
Why are animals yellow? / Melissa Stewart.
p. cm. — (Rainbow of animals)
Includes bibliographical references.
Summary: "Uses examples of animals in the wild to explain why some animals are yellow"—Provided by publisher.
ISBN 978-0-7660-3253-8
1. Animals—Color—Juvenile literature. 2. Yellow—Juvenile literature. I. Title.
QL767.S75 2009
591.47'2—dc22 2008011474

ISBN-10: 0-7660-3253-1

Printed in the United States of America

10 9 8 7 6 5 4 3 2 1

To Our Readers: We have done our best to make sure all Internet Addresses in this book were active and appropriate when we went to press. However, the author and the publisher have no control over and assume no liability for the material available on those Internet sites or on other Web sites they may link to. Any comments or suggestions can be sent by e-mail to comments@enslow.com or to the address on the back cover.

♻ Enslow Publishers, Inc., is committed to printing our books on recycled paper. The paper in every book contains 10% to 30% post-consumer waste (PCW). The cover board on the outside of each book contains 100% PCW. Our goal is to do our part to help young people and the environment too!

Every effort has been made to locate all copyright holders of material used in this book. If any errors or omissions have occurred, corrections will be made in future editions of this book.

All photos by Minden Pictures:
Interior: © Adrian Davies/npl, pp. 6–7, 28 (butterfly); © Barry Mansell/npl, p. 5 (frog); © Bren Hedges/npl, pp. 22–23, 29 (sea dragon); © Chris Newbert, p. 4 (boxfish); © Frans Lanting, p. (katydid); © Fred Bavendam, pp. 1 (bottom left), 12–13, 26, 28 (pufferfish), 29 (frogfish) © Gerry Ellis, pp. 18–19, 29 (lion); © Hans Cristoph Kappel/npl, p. 5 (butterfly); © Ing Arndt/Foto Natura, pp. 1 (top left), 8–9, 28 (caterpillars); © Konrad Wothe, pp. 14–15, 28 (bee) © Michael & Patricia Fogden, pp. 1 (top right), 27, 29 (viper); © Michael Durham, pp. 24, 2 (owl); © Michael Quinton, pp. 20–21, 29 (goose); © Pete Oxford, p. 4 (chameleon); © Ren Krekels/Foto Natura, pp. 10–11, 28 (salamander); © S & D & K Maslowski/FLPA, pp. 1 (bottom right), 16–17, 28 (bird); © Tom Vezo, p. 4 (cardinal).
Cover: (clockwise from top left) © Ingo Arndt/Foto Natura; © Michael & Patricia Fogden © S & D & K Maslowski/FLPA; © Fred Bavendam.

Illustration Credits: © 1999, Artville, LLC, pp. 28–29 (maps).

Note to Parents and Teachers: The *Rainbow of Animals* series supports the National Scienc Education Standards for K–4 science. The Words to Know section introduces subject-specifi vocabulary words, including pronunciation and definitions. Early readers may need help wit these new words.

Answers to the Guessing Game:

The yellow body of a sargassum frogfish blends in with the seaweed that lives in its watery world.

An eyelash viper lives in deep, dark rain forests. But its bright colors can still help it hide from enemies. The viper blends in with the yellow fruits in the tree.

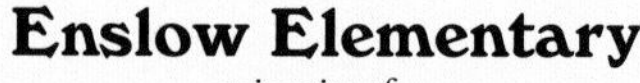

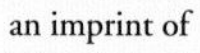

Enslow Publishers, Inc.
40 Industrial Road
Box 398
Berkeley Heights, NJ 07922
USA

http://www.enslow.com